WHEN GOD FALLS IN LOVE

WHEN GOD FALLS IN LOVE

(poetry)

Oluwatosin Olabode Samson

Oluwatosin Olabode Samson

Copyright ©2018 Oluwatosin Olabode Samson

ISBN: 978-978-965-994-4

All rights reserved.
No part of this book may be reproduced, distributed, stored in a retrieval system, or transmitted, in any form or by any means, electronic, electrostatic, magnetic tape, mechanical, photocopying, recording, or otherwise without prior written permission from the Publisher.
For information about permission to reproduce selections from this book, write to info@wrr.ng

National Library of Nigeria Cataloguing-in-Publication Data

Cover Design: Akila Jibrin

Printed and Published in Nigeria by:
Words Rhymes & Rhythm Limited
Suite C309, Global Plaza Plot 366, Obafemi Awolowo Way, Jabi District, Abuja, Nigeria.
08169027757, 08060109295
www.wrr.ng

CONTENTS

DEDICATION 7
INTRODUCTION 8
THE BIBLE AND THE HUMAN RACE....................9
WHAT GRACE DOES.......................................12
GLORY 14
MY EVERYTHING..16
THE SOVEREIGN BEING 17
MORE THAN JUST A WORD............................18
WHAT'S MOST IMPORTANT? 21
AS GENTLE AS A DOVE..................................22
I LIVE TO WORSHIP YOU 23
FOREVER WITH JESUS...................................25
YOUTH AGE 26
NOT HOLDING BACK 28
MAKE ME...30
JEALOUSY 31
CHRISTMAS..32
I BECAME ONE – A PROSTITUTE 33
WHEN GOD FALLS IN LOVE 37
THIS SHOULD NOT BE SO 39
TO WHOM DO YOU REPENT?........................40
HAVE ME BACK!...41
PROCRASTINATION 43
CONFESSIONS..44
ONE 46

I WANT A CHRIST-LIKE LOVE	47
GUESS WHO WAS BORN	48
I'M GRATEFUL	50
JESUS	51
MAN	53
MAKE YOUR MOTIVE RIGHT	55
INSURED BLOOD	57
FORMALLY SUICIDAL	59
A THOUGHT	61
THE UNSTOPPABLE	62
HALLELUIAH!	63
HUMAN RACE	64

DEDICATION

To everyone who has and who will come to the knowledge of God's Love.

INTRODUCTION

When God fell in love,
He didn't just think it, he acted.
His action saved humanity forever
and not just His Thought.
Your strength isn't in what you think.
Your active strength is in what you do.

It's a waste to think and never
implement.

— **Oluwatosin Olabode Samson**

THE BIBLE AND THE HUMAN RACE

      I.
Just because Yesterday
was once that Today's Tomorrow
two days ago gave man the pseudo confidence
to snub the fear of the morrow
and lure us to forget that
not only had we never seen her;
we may be gone when the morrow comes.

We sleep at night
surrendering to the taming hands of nature
'cause somewhere in the White House of our minds,
we believe Tomorrow will come
    saying *'it would and should come anyways'*.
So we plan for the future
and not THE END.

*YET we call them **'stupid'**
who believe in an 'Invisible God'.*

      II.
Daily, we hear of accidents and death;
    it's no longer news.
Undeterred... we travel about as men of faith,
    trusting that the dexterous hands of
    our chauffeur
    will steer us safely to our destinations;
forget not... some didn't yesterday to the morrow we
are in today.
    *We still trust those hands today
    since the journey (of life) must continue.*

We sit like sardines in public vehicles
with our body massaging other's bodies
knowing not if the 'gentleman' on the right,
or 'quiet' one on the left
carries within, a malignant soul –
> a kidnapper
> a serial killer
> a rapist...

So we sit and sleep,
planning for the future unseen,
unafraid, because we trust them.

*YET we call them **'stupid'***
who put their trust in an 'Invisible God'.

III.
We live in perilous times
of senseless violence and sudden disasters
but in this jungle of life
the hustle in hunt for daily meal
continues amidst this turbulence.
We walk the jungle (of life) as though immune
to the poisonous bites stings of world.

YET, he is an **idiot**
who believes in the complete Truth

IV.
I look at all these and
saw our Ignorance dancing in the garment of
'enlightenment'
while we're despising one another

in satisfaction with *'incomplete Truths'*

Have you paused to consider this:
    that which you have labelled irrelevant
    in your twenty first century wisdom
    is the mortar that welded the bricks of the
    nineteenth century

So when you say, *'Let's keep updating'*
I say, *'the BIBLE needs no **updating'***
And you say, *'That's a book full of crap!'*
I say a prayer for you
to the 'Invisible God'.

WHAT GRACE DOES

Grace is a call to surrender
and not a stimulant for further blunder.
It is the intention of the Cross
not the product of our works.

                          Grace is Christ's bleeding
                                for our forgiveness
                            for the remission of our sins
                 active upon a conscious cooperative act:
                                        G.R.A.C.E

Grace is the evidence of His power
Our role is to enjoy by yielding to His Will.
Not that we deserve it
but for His compassion and care.

                              Grace is the opener that
                 un-cork the bottles of our understanding
              and blows up our mind like blooming flowers
           for the comprehension of the beauty of wisdom,
                  that the jury in our hearts may be learned
                  enough to adjudge that which is evil or good.

Grace opens man to the reality
which God's love presents to us.
Through Christ are we sanctified
as worthy souls who're qualified
to be called 'Sons'.

                            Grace sanctifies for Purpose,
                          Grace beautifies your Essence,
                          Grace erases man's selfishness

and teaches the 'art' of selflessness.

Grace is the mother that birth
Man's communion with the Father.
And freed us from the shackles
of sin and of death
of the old nature and evil depth.

Grace changes us
Grace humbles us
Grace uplifts us
to realms above and beyond

Grace is a divine dictionary
that unravels Life's meaning
in the abode of His divine Help.

Grace is the core of our existence!

Oluwatosin Olabode Samson

GLORY

I believe in You, my God.
I have confidence in You.
My faith brews in your Being.

I see you in my past.
I see you as my future.
your thoughts inhabit my dreams.

I know you've been calling...
I hear you, now, in loud silence,
HERE I AM!

Jesus! My royal Highness.
You are Beauty, Glory;
you are Holiness, Magnificence.

Four and twenty elders prostrate
    like the resplendent angels,
They sing in awe of your Glory

Glory! Glory!! Glory!!!
We are your creation,
we exist for your glory

You are Light,
brighter than the sun –
    the Light of the Son.

You are worthy.
You are glorious!
Heavens sing your praise.

I see light,
I see your Light.
I see your Light in my darkness...

MY EVERYTHING

He's my everything,
The reason I live,
The reason I breathe,
The reason for my reasons.

From conception to death,
He's the fulfillment in-between,
He's the king, my ruler,
He's the leader, my Father.

He's creation's creator
Filled with wisdom and might,
His words are life,
His presence glory.

He's my everything,
He knows me by name,
Has me on his palm
I live to worship Him.

He's amazing and eternally the same.

THE SOVEREIGN BEING

Who is man
   an ordinary being
      that you would punish yourself
         for his sins and helplessness?

Who is man
   that you are mindful of him
      constantly revealing yourself to him
         and delighting your heart
           in his knowledge of you?

         You are sovereign
       why not just command him?

You are God!
   Who is man
      that you give him the liberty of choice?
      Could you not just bend him
         under the weight of your fist?

         Who is this man
      that you couldn't speak 'into being'?

Who is man
   that you forged him from dust
      mere mud brought to life
         in your likeness
           to rule and have dominion?

      Man is but your ambassador,
      Man is nothing in himself,
      Man is nothing without you.

MORE THAN JUST A WORD

I.
You see
When I first began this mission
I swore nothing could cloud my vision
For I knew that I had all the provisions
To manifest the yearnings of my passions

Still relevant were my imperfections
Yes, I was full of erroneous repetitions
Even though I had full blown confessions
That she would remain my eternal mission

I was set to make a difference,
But selfishness overcame me
And things began to present themselves differently

II.
You see
The change came from me
It didn't come from anything else
But the man in me had become different
And indeed indifferent!

Like fractions
We began dividing our future actions
And apologizing for each subtractions
As we floated on *Cloud 9* to subjections

And then it all became so rocky
That I feared for the present because
The past wouldn't let go
Even though the future smelled rosy

III.
You see
when we first started out
I had a pretty good definition of my position
So when we fell, we blamed it on time
We grew distant and blamed it on distance

Soon we lost touch for the fear the
Communication gaps we couldn't account for
Believe me, we were once truly in love
But lost lust took it away from us

Ah, if I could turn back the hands of time...
I wouldn't exit my comfort zone to please you
I wouldn't try to be someone else for you
I wouldn't feed my obsession to be with you

IV.
You see
If I could turn back the hands of time
I wouldn't love you more or less
I would be selfish –
for us, not for me

If I could turn back the hands of time
our love would be blind, but I promise
we would mend shortcomings with corrections
encouraging us to not take notes

My love, since the hands of time are too firm to be
turned back
I pray that the future us will fall in love with one less

>   mistake
> For now I I've learnt this fact:
> *'I love you'* is more than just a word

WHAT'S MOST IMPORTANT?

What is most important?

It's the time you invest
Not the by-products of thoughts
It's the company you keep
Not the gifts you give.

What is most important?

It's not the comfort of life you give
It's the comfort you share
It's not your accomplishments
Noted by your absence.

What is most important?

It's never found in doing
It is what you do in 'being'
It's never in "I thought"
It's always an 'I know'.

What is most important?

Let not your assets
Spend more time with your loved ones
Than you do with them
Create time for the ones you love.

Oluwatosin Olabode Samson

AS GENTLE AS A DOVE

If you can give into thoughts without fighting
Or would listen to the words of wisdom without pride
If you can smile and laugh without faking
And can be contented because you need to.

If you can be reasonable while trying to reason
Or be considerate when things don't go as you expected
If you can forget to fault friends when they have earned it
Or would remember to forgive when they don't deserve it

If you can accept people for their industrious nature
And not take it as arrogance or competition
If you can be objective about constructive criticism
Without mounting walls of defense

If you honestly wouldn't condemn anyone
Because that's not who you are
If you wouldn't worry about what you'll eat
and wouldn't curse when you have nothing to eat

Then, Dear human
You are almost as good as a dove!
And Peace is possible,
if only we all could be as gentle as a dove.

I LIVE TO WORSHIP YOU

Joy
Undoubted assurance
Warmth; Serenity
This is what I feel in you.
Your mercies are
New every morning.

Yes, Father
I hear You.
I see the Truth.
Lord, I see You
I feel Your Spirit
That is why I'm here.

In a glimpse of You, I capture my essence
And grasp my nature.
As the world becomes obscure
Leaving me in Your presence
Abiding under Your shadow,
The place of peace.

Here, in your presence
the pestilence becomes calm
And in that still moment
I know You
I know You, my God
Will make it flow like a river.

I lift my hands in worship
My soul cries out
It proclaims Your Lordship
To the ends of the earth.

Oluwatosin Olabode Samson

I let myself completely loose in You
And my heart sings.

And so
I behold your Face.
Of your promises
In your Word,
Lord, I live
To worship You.

FOREVER WITH JESUS

I'll worship you forever and ever
though it may not be the standard
It would be to the best I can offer.

I really do love you
In my crappy human way
Yet I feel unworthy of you.

Lord, help me to remain
The image of you
Loving you as best as I can.

Lord, I am grateful always
For You being You
And making me, me.

Jesus, I've searched all through
And found only you to be true
I surrender myself.

Have your way with me
For it seems I cannot handle myself
Alone without you.

YOUTH AGE

It's time to make mistakes
It's time for us to grow
When dreams are big
And desires unending.

> *"Allow me, dear world, to explore*
> *Allow me live out my life*
> *And do all I love to do"*.

Tic... tic... tic...

Time sounds on
It waits not for anyone
Tomorrow will make me older
With no interest for the things of yesterday.

The youth age
Forget what others may say
Become who you were created to be
For with each moment demands another lifestyle

Not just the person the world approves
For there is no limit to your greatness
Unless you agree otherwise
To be swept under the carpet.

You are beautiful
You are beautiful
It doesn't hurt to know this
Believe it to be true.

I am a youth
I have a thousand questions
Life distracts me easily
I revel in assumed wisdom.

I pride in ignorance
I desire all that I imagine
And need not all I want.
I am just a youth.

Stalk not my flaws
For, as you seek to point them out
You must give my stalk a breathing space
To G.R.O.W!

So next time you feel like stealing my youth
    (though speaking words of truth
    about the failings of my life)
Help me to G.R.O.W also
For this is the youth age.

NOT HOLDING BACK

Philippians 4:13

With my eyes on Jesus
Nothing can hold me back
Trials and temptation might try
And sometimes even win small battles
But nothing holds me back.

I've been through thick and thin
I've survived ups and down
I've explored multifarious existence
And my eyes are still set on Jesus
So nothing holds me back.

Oh yes! I know I do not know all
But I must confess this truth:
I've been told a lie, and then the truth
That I may set my eyes on sure targets
Not deceit without a sure direction.

No!
This time I walk with sure vision
Seeing the invisible plainly
My passion burns like flames
It feeds on the knowledge of God.

I say goodbye to my ignorance
And the moments I could have done better
But settled for less – holding back
Wanting to do everything on my own
Without a goal of my own.

Those days have gone
For I have discovered Jesus
His words in Philippians 4:13 –
'Doing all things through Christ that strengthens me'
I work and walk in His strength.

So nothing is going to hold me back
As Christ and I team up in victory!
I have a mission
To fully achieve
I am not holding back!

MAKE ME

Lord, make me a man of humility
Whose pride is in the death and
Resurrection of our Lord
And Savior –*Jesus Christ.*

And I'll worship you
In truth and in spirit
And bless your name eternally
Till my breath leaves me.

Lord, make me a woman of 'conscious beauty
Whose dignity is rooted in Christ' compassion
And I'll value my essence
Beyond make-up and human approvals.

Make me a child of obedience
Whose 'rush' in life is in the
Sacrifice of patience and self-control
To wisely follow You in life.

JEALOUSY

Jealousy is dangerous
It can kill you
Alter your focus
Change your direction
And leave you cluttered.

Jealousy tasks you
Until you have no time for yourself
It leaves you empty, always hoping
Your trust isn't stolen
Suddenly, you become isolated!

Oh! The pain of a jealous lover
Who sits on a cushion of distrust
And keeps the lover in mind –
Worrying, wondering and conjuring
The sins of the past on suspicion's canvas.

Jealousy is poison
It breeds envy
And fuels anger
As it casts the foundation
Of a broken relationship.

Do not court jealousy
Where you can be open
For the troubled dust of the mind
Can only be settled through knowledge
That comes from two.

CHRISTMAS

Christmas is that seed of kindness
The homeless you clothe
The hungry you feed
The sinner you didn't judge
The prayers, not curses you offer.

Christmas is Jesus
His attributes make it worthwhile
The feeling of a new joy birthed
And the luster of overwhelming praise
Laced with grace for all our days.

I BECAME ONE – A PROSTITUTE

Among many that had me
Are evil desires
Passion of the flesh
Which lowers my nature.

My soul panted after her
'I just couldn't resist her'
'Give it a try', I thought!
Its pleasure and doesn't hurt.

Lust!
For the price of love
I gave my beauty away.
I gave my beauty away
like vegetable that'd lose
nutrients in a single rinse.

Temptation isn't overwhelming
When it's with the unloved
Like Joseph with Potiphar's wife
But when it comes to the one with whom you see a future
The one your heart is already committed to
It's most assuredly… not easy.

With this excuse, I fell…
I let loose my guard.
I become one, while becoming one flesh…
My licentiousness had me;
It was fun, I must confess.
So, it happened again and again.

What's painful is, I claimed to be a Christian.
Flirting with every chance I got
while remaining a brother/sister outwardly.
All the while... thinking
With grace it's just a normal thing.
More so, we've got 'something' going on
And God's forgiveness shall abound.

Man Speaking
I'm only human
I've tried to stay single, faithful
But...
> Her two soft mountains,
> Fully grown and well-shaped
> ...His chest, giving me that soothing, comforting and safe feeling
> ...Her lower lips, my gosh!
> ... His scent releasing dopamine smell... oh my!

> '... Have me, they kept calling, 'just one more...'
> ...just one more...

Too good a feeling to be
A step closer to condemnation.

Though I lost calibration with the Lord,
He didn't leave without a fight.
For the 'joy' set before me
I was blinded to righteousness.

This heart freezing feeling respects no human.
This feelings infest you in spite of the immorality anti-viruses
Preinstalled by the church or your parents
On your mind

Call it whatever you will:
> *Fornication, adultery, obscenity*
> *Pornography, concupiscence, rape*
> *Orgy, homosexuality or incest.*

All the same, it will kill you
Maybe not now, but definitely in eternity

God Speaking
When you reach out to me
I do not spit your past all over you.
My time is better spent
Discussing your 'present' and your 'future'.

I will forgive.
Just decide, dear child, to come back home.
You've tried on your own already, remember?
But it was to no avail.

Just come back home.
Like any other
I'll forgive and grant you peace.
I'm waiting for you my royal priesthood.

Connect through my ever-working grace
It's my strength to weaken hindrances to your race.

Man Speaking
Now with God
I am no longer a Prostitute;
My past is over. Thanks to Jesus.
I'm walking in God's grace
by the leading of His Holy Spirit.
Not just me, you certainly can too!

WHEN GOD FALLS IN LOVE

When God is in love with you
There isn't anything you can do about it
He fantasizes about you all day long
Writing your name on his palm in rosy fonts daily
And counting the strands of your hair
As though he has become jobless for your sake.
Indeed, it is all because nothing else is
More important than you to Him

When God is in love with you
There isn't anything you can do about it
He will give and never stop giving
Though there is nothing to get back from you
He will blush and gush over you
And call you 'the one after my heart'
When God is in love with you
His omnipresence manifests around you
And, no matter what, he never leaves

When God is in love with you
There isn't anything you can do about it
He is constantly mindful of you
He reminds you that you are
Fearfully and wonderfully made in His Image
Under his care, you will glow and shine
Radiating auspiciously with a glory
too peaceful and joyful for the world to comprehend

Do not doubt when God says 'I love you'
Do not think yourself too messed up
For it is not who you have become that matters to Him
But who you are – *His original creation!*

Oluwatosin Olabode Samson

His Grace, Mercy and Forgiveness will cover you
It is no wonder then that He never says
'I once loved you' or 'I love you no more'

When God is in love with you
There isn't anything you can do about it

Guess what?
He is already in love with you

Yes, YOU!

THIS SHOULD NOT BE SO

It's in bad times
that I forget You
>   – *When things turn upside down and
>   unfaithfulness becomes my friend.*

Why me?
Couldn't it have been anyone else?
At least I know I'm better than most!

It is in bad times
That I forget you
>   – *Your faithfulness becomes vague*

It is easier to put the blame on...
... but you said
Your word – thinking like man, is a lie
Your righteousness put to question

It is in bad times
That I forget You
>   – *I really do forget You*

But, I've come to realize now
That this should not be so
For God's faithfulness is consistent
As fervent in bad times
As it is in good times

Oluwatosin Olabode Samson

TO WHOM DO YOU REPENT?

You say, *'I repent... I repent... I repent'*.
But to whom do you repent? Your conscience?

You say, 'my *gosh! I feel so bad*
Just how did I end up like this?'
But to whom do you repent? To your 'self'?

You say, *'I repent... I repent... I repent'*
But to whom do you repent?

You say, *'Lord, I'm sorry'*
Yet like a dog, you return to your vomit.
You say, *'Lord it won't happen again'*
But you're soon back in the pit

You say, *'I repent... I repent... I repent'*.
But to whom do you repent?

Is your heart speaking to Jesus?
Are you seeking His face?
Are you humbly confessing your sins?
Are you turning from your evil ways?

Do you repent unto Jesus?
Or are your confessions gratifying 'self'?
Is it game to relieve yourself from guilt?

If your words are indeed unto Jesus
He will permanently take the guilt away
His specialty is in making old things new

HAVE ME BACK!

Dear Jesus,
I miss You, I love You
I desperately need You

I drifted away
But I've heard Your call
And I want to return

You're my first love
And I still get butterflies
Just thinking about You.

Lost, I am grateful
That You didn't lose me to death
You lost me to life

Life and its trappings distracted me
And I always thought I was living
But something was always missing

I never admitted it
But, deep down, I knew something was missing
Even Google couldn't find it

Lord Jesus, you are everything to me
And I now know
I'm nothing without You.

Take me back Jesus
I come ready this time
I have no shame

Oluwatosin Olabode Samson

Yes, Jesus I'll be Yours
Just please have me back
This time, I am for real!

PROCRASTINATION

My accomplishments
    are as fulfilling
        as my procrastinations
            which is a fool-feeling.

I've got goals –
    goals unto greatness
        they are waiting on the day
            I'll follow them.

When shall I stop this
    fool-feeling of procrastination
        and start fulfilling my dreams
            by the power of my actions?

CONFESSIONS

I.
I am addicted to confessions
So much that I deserve to be tagged a guru
    for I say my sorries expertly

                          Forgive me, conscience
                    For I've sinned against my soul

I am allergic to guilt moods –
    mood swings don't do well with me
So I apologize and say I'm sorry
Over and over again after my fall into a pool of regret

I am only addicted to confessions
Remorse has always been my tool
But repentance is a scarce commodity
...and the way I say my *sorries* –
    so expertly that it shocks me too
I know there is strong hold on me
    'I thought I had dealt with this already'

II.
    I am addicted to sin
                  I am allergic to God

I want nothing to do with either
But, oh! Both are so strongly contagious
So I am torn in two by my guilt pleasure –
I neither want to stop nor want to continue
I fight a battle within, conscious of nothing else

One minute confession falls from my lips

Remorse spills down my eyes…
Then, all of a sudden I have done it again!
Oh my God! What the heck!
Alas, the euphoria of confession is a paper tiger

III.
People like me are believed to be sold out
To the Higher Being, and their eyes look at us
As perfect saints above the failings of flesh

But sin can pleasure in many forms
And, though I may be so somewhat shy in public
My sins express themselves in my privacy
Passionately and permanently

But these secret acts never believed…

IV.
We fight our flesh
    With our hearts
        Worked up
            Angered
                Feeling the kiss of danger
                      And the tight hug of regret
                With less, and lesser confidence
            To approach the Father

We are in so much pain
We confess to consciousness
To regain a slice of peace

We repent – *but only to self*
We are addicted to confession!

ONE

You can only be one –
    the idea you
    control by self-decisions
        or the result of what your
        society makes of you

                Here's a clue:

        the real you emerges
        when you are alone and shielded
        from the judging eyes of the world

        the fake you is the one
        that crawls out of you like a worm
        when you face the world

You can only be one –
    the idea you
    control by self-decisions
        or the result of what your
        society makes of you

        Pick the one to which your life belongs!

I WANT A CHRIST-LIKE LOVE

I want a type of love that wouldn't grow weak
the type that wouldn't fade like fake wall paints
I want that type of love that is free and fearless
the one that wouldn't have to hide its emotions

I seek a love that wouldn't float on self-gratification
the type that wouldn't play hurtful games
I seek a love that burns with passion, like wild fire
the type that doesn't blind itself to the future

I want love blind to friend's 'how to love' manuals
the type that is unique, fresh, real and genuine
I want love that is truthful and respectful
the type that finds strength in mutual understanding

>Come, and share of my love
>the type where I can:
>
>Kiss your doubts
>   cuddle your pains
>   hug your fears
>   sort your frustrations
>   share your happiness

I want pure love –
simple and Christ-like!

GUESS WHO WAS BORN

I.
It was told by an angel
He would be called Emmanuel
Conceived of the Holy Spirit
Born as the Son of God.

Mary, a precious virgin
And Joseph, a fortunate fellow
Were the blessed vessels
Used by God to bring the wonderful Savior
For the salvation of humanity

Guess who was born?
The clues are simple
He came and was crucified
Now you can point Him to your situation
And get resolution by His authority

II.
Revelation says
He's coming, again, for His bride
He has paid the bride price already
With the hard currency of His blood
He paid once for all of humanity
We called it salvation

Will you be one of his brides?
Destined for Eternal Life in His Kingdom?
You can, if you wish to be
And the qualification is simple
Just say a 'Yes' to his proposal

III.
So, can you guess who was born?
It is He's who Was, Is and Will Be:
He was born
And will be born
In you, in me, in all of us
I pray He's born in your heart today
Merry Christmas!
Jesus is born!

I AM GRATEFUL

He stands with me through thick and thin
Because He loves me, not because I'm worthy
Even I know that I am not good enough

                It has been so many years of pain
             I, sweating over hopeless works of shame
       Yet those who surround me have nothing to gain
        My poor self bears the heavy weight of blame

          Life becomes harder with each passing day
       So much hard that I have long given up on me
         But He stands with me through thick and thin
        Because He loves me, not because I'm worthy

          I'm grateful, for, with You, I am a better me
              You daily forge a better version of me
                 Relaxed, calm, at peace, productive
            Even I know that I am not good enough

          Lord, I am forever grateful for Your Grace
             My sins were many, foul like a pigsty
            Now, I live a new life because of You
       I really am grateful for your Redeeming Love

He stands with me through thick and thin
Because He loves me, not because I'm worthy
Even I know that I am not good enough

JESUS

He's the one for whom the world was created
Whether in heaven or on earth
Whether principalities or powers
Whether visible or invisible
He is the sum of all creation.

He's the one that founded
The foundation of the earth in the air
And separated the sky from the ground
Without any pillar
To hold the firmament

He's the careful God
Who has made me full of care
So faithful
He made me full of faith
In His divine resurrection

His focus was on His essence
And not people's expectation in His presence
He was called a carpenter's son
With low life birthed in Bethlehem
Yet, He made scholars to wonder

Religious folks waited
For His church showcase
Yet, His first miracle was at a party
He was the one – a Jew
Who exalted Samaritans in the presence of critics

A Holy Man who hung around sinners
And ate with a tax collector

Oluwatosin Olabode Samson

There is no one like Him
A man whose presence is royalty
Yet lived outside its very comfort

He has victories over death
Champion of Calvary
He is the Resurrection
And the Life
Lamb of God

He is the Living Water
The Way to the Father
Milk for children
Meat for men
husband of the widow

He's the one who
Created us for community
Designed us for destiny
Fashioned us for fellowship
He is the one above all else

A God of several chances
Not just a God of second chance
He is Jesus
The way, the truth, the life –
The Son of the living God!

MAN

Who is man?
An ordinary being
That You a supreme being
Would punish Yourself
For his sins and helplessness?

Who is man
That you are mindful of him?
That You constantly
Describe Yourself to him
Just so he can get to know You?

Who is this man?
Wouldn't You just command him?
Wouldn't You just enforce your will?
You are God
Why give him free will?

Who is man
That he had to be fearfully created?
That he had to be wonderfully created?
That You had to bend down to dust
And in the mud, mold him to life?

Who is this man
That you wouldn't just speak into being?
That You had to make him in Your Image
In Your likeness
To rule and have dominion?

Man is but
A pleasure to You

Oluwatosin Olabode Samson

Your love and family
Your representative
Your Son's children

Man is nothing in himself
But the one You choose
To lavish Your love upon
Man is everything in You
Man is nothing without You

Who is a man?

MAKE YOUR MOTIVE RIGHT

God Speaking:

>Whom do I give My inheritance
>When I can't call you son?
>Though you claim to know Me
>All I can say is 'I never knew you'
>
>Depart! You worker of iniquity
>The world affirms you as being religious
>Doing all so your self may be glorified
>When My glory is for Me alone
>
>Yeah, you cast out the demons
>Your ministry is laid on signs and wonders
>Your speech has allowed the Holy Spirit win souls
>You know scripture better than the Pope
>You are a teacher of the law...
>But I never knew you!
>
>Your every good deed
>May be a starting point to salvation
>For those with whom you reach out to
>It is but a reward for you.
>Only in Jesus is your salvation found
>Not what you seemingly do for Him
>It is from Him that Light shines on His sons
>
>I never knew you
>For you called Me Lord but never made Me yours
>You came to my works but never came to Me
>You came into My Kingdom but settled for every other thing I had to offer.

You still have now
To ponder my words
Make your motive right
Introduce Me to your heart
Preach Me to others
And be an evidence of Grace
Before you face Me on the Day of Judgment

INSURED BLOOD

What will be done has been done
Entering into an existence
That has already existed
Living and doing things
That have already been done
Concerning this
It cannot be mistaken
If It follows His way

The insured blood
No more, no less
Couldn't give anything else
While the world's system
Is seeking confirmation
This one – yes, already confirmed
It's a life free from doubt
Certain of what life's about

It's no longer me living
But Christ living in me
He is perfect
A state I am becoming
In which all things become new
As I let go, old things passing away
My blood's insured too
As he now lives in me

The insured blood
I got when I dwell in Him
My protection always assured
It's strength not from the future
It's always in the present

To be insured is to be certain
That He in whom I have my being
Has covered all I could have thought of.

As His word says
Without the shedding of blood
There cannot be forgiveness of sins
His blood was given and it satisfies all
But only when insured to you
Only the insured blood
Keeps you whole enough
To return to Him saved.

FORMALLY SUICIDAL

Have you ever been depressed?

I'm lost in myself
I feel there is a bomb in me
It is ticking towards an explosive end
Does anyone care to know?

I'm bored by this life
Even suicide seems refreshing
It's an easy way out
Better than to face this evil torture
It wasn't always like this

You may call these excuses
Yes, tell me I'm indulging in self-pity, I know
But I find myself wrapped in it
I feel alone and lonely

Can anyone hear me?
Can anyone hear the ticking bomb?
Who's out there to save me?
Please can anyone hear me?
I'm really dying!

Save me now!
Help me take this bomb out
Before you begin to read about me in past tense
I'm letting you know now
Please don't ignore me!

YOU WERE THERE

You were there
You were there always
God, you've been faithful
You've been awesome

You are there
You've always been there
There has been understanding
Natural connections
Some to be grown into
All because you were there

A THOUGHT

People are God's creation
Created for worship
To worship beyond religion
In a religion that understands relationship

Our essence is to exhale
What Christ inhaled into us
Which is a life
beyond imaginations.

Understanding the essence of our existence
Makes us realize the purpose of His importance
And understand that He does not mind circumstances
To define the distance between him and his chance.

WHAT A MIGHTY GOD WE SERVE!

What a Mighty God we serve!
They can't hold Him
You can't hold Him either
All it takes is to know Him
And you will be certain

Creation is here to attest to this
Angels are always praising
The Elders are worshipping
Everything He does, He does well
What a Mighty God we serve!

Reasoning with common sense
He took something that was messed up
And made a wonderful me *out of it*
He's awesome, glorious and spectacular
He's special, He's a Mighty God!

There's no other god above Him
Compared to Him, there's no other
He's the Ancient of days, not dependent on time
He's a friend, closer than a brother
He's a Mighty God, has always and will always be.

HALLELUIAH!

Once upon a time
Man in all his glory was amazing
There was no jungle justice
All was moving smoothly

Then came the villain
and all hope seemed lost
in the deceit of what looked good
we fell and blamed it on him

Our peace was taken away
without any intimacy
Man in the same skin
Was all naked and ashamed

But like a movie script
just when the villain thought he had it all
Christ showed up!
Crucifixion was His game plan

The villain laughed, mocked and spat
what he didn't know was that
Three days later
Resurrection is the victory

Halleluiah!

HUMAN RACE

Hello everybody
my name is *Human Race*
but my friends call me
people of the world

Something happened to me
On the day of my conception
That's held me guilty
Until the day of grace

At the point of insertion
My initiation into this sinful world began
At that faithful moment
The journey from freedom to find freedom began

So for nine months
I was in the storage room
Downloading data spanning
time past into *time to come*

Data sufficient enough
To lead me back
Then I arrived
Completely equipped to return

When God Falls in Love

www.ingramcontent.com/pod-product-compliance
Lightning Source LLC
Chambersburg PA
CBHW051350040426
42453CB00007B/499